1-2-3 Draw
Ocean Life

A step-by-step guide

by
Freddie Levin

Peel Productions, Inc
Columbus, NC

Before you begin, you will need:

- a pencil
- an eraser
- a pencil sharpener
- a ruler
- lots of paper (recycle and re-use)
- colored pencils for finished drawings
- a folder for saving your work
- a good light
- a comfortable place to draw

Now, let's begin!

Library of Congress Cataloging-in-Publication Data

Levin, Freddie.
    1-2-3 draw ocean life : a step-by-step guide / by Freddie Levin.
        p. cm. -- (1-2-3 draw)
    Includes bibliographical references and index.
    ISBN 0-939217-62-7 (sewn paper binding : alk. paper)
1. Marine animals in art--Juvenile literature. 2. Drawing--Technique--Juvenile literature. I. Title: Ocean life. II. Title: One-two-three draw ocean life. III. Title. IV. Series.

NC781.L48 2005
743.6'177--dc22

2004024504

Printed September 2010
Print run# 000125025

by: Stone Sapphire (HK) Limited
        No.608 Xinzhai Road
        Sheshan Town, Songjiang District
        Shanghai, China

for: Books are Fun
        282 Century Place, Suite 2000
        Louisville, CO 80027
        Tel. 303-516-3400

Contents

Important Drawing Tips:

1 Draw lightly at first (SKETCH!), so you can erase extra lines later.

2 The first few shapes are important. Notice the placement, sizes and positions of the first shapes.

3 Practice, practice, practice!

4 Have fun drawing ocean life!

Basic shapes

All the ocean creatures in this book start with a basic shape.
Practice drawing these shapes:

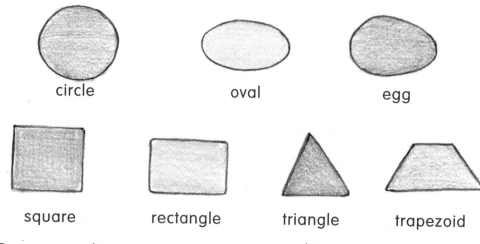

circle   oval   egg

square rectangle triangle trapezoid

Do you see things around you that might start with these basic shapes?

Fish vocabulary

Let's learn the names of some parts of a fish. It will make it easier to show you how to draw one.

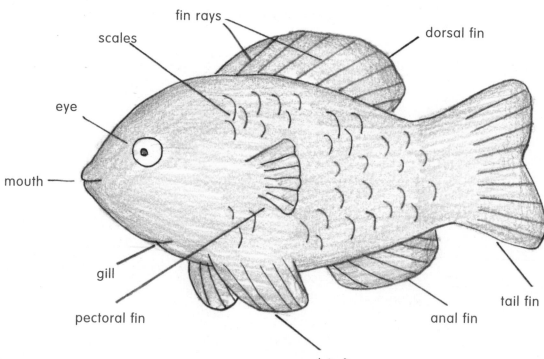

fin rays

scales

dorsal fin

eye

mouth

gill

pectoral fin

pelvic fin

anal fin

tail fin

About oceans

If you were in a space ship, looking down at Earth, you would see a beautiful blue planet. Oceans cover more than two-thirds of the Earth. These oceans are filled with all sorts of creatures. Some are tiny, some are huge. Some are brightly colored, and some are strange and mysterious. This book contains only a small part of these interesting ocean creatures.

To learn more about ocean life, check out the books at your public or school library.

Note to parents and teachers:

This book is designed to help the young artist break down complicated images into simple shapes and to see the relationships between the shapes.

Starting is sometimes the hardest part!

To encourage children who are very young, have little confidence or poorly developed motor control, cut some circles and ovals out of tag board. Have the child move these shapes into position on drawing paper and trace around the shapes to get the first step of each drawing.

Dolphin

(6 to 13 feet long)

A dolphin is not a fish. It is a mammal that lives in the ocean. Mammals give birth and nurse their babies. A dolphin uses its tail to swim. Playful, friendly dolphins come to the surface and breathe air through their blow holes. They communicate in a language of clicks and squeaks.

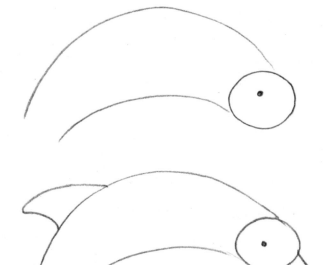

1 Look at the shapes and lines in the first drawing. Lightly sketch a small circle for the head. Draw a small eye. Start the dolphin's body with two curved lines.

2 Draw the dolphin's snout. It's called a 'beak.' Add a dorsal fin.

3 Draw two flippers. Using curved lines, add the tail.

4 Look at the final drawing. Erase extra sketch lines. Shade and color your dolphin.

Orca, or Killer Whale

(up to 23 feet long)

Like dolphins, whales are ocean mammals. There are two types of whales: toothed and baleen. Toothed whales like Orcas have teeth and hunt seals, penguins, and turtles for their dinner. Baleen whales eat tiny plants and animals called plankton (see page 27). They sift them into their mouths through screens called baleens.

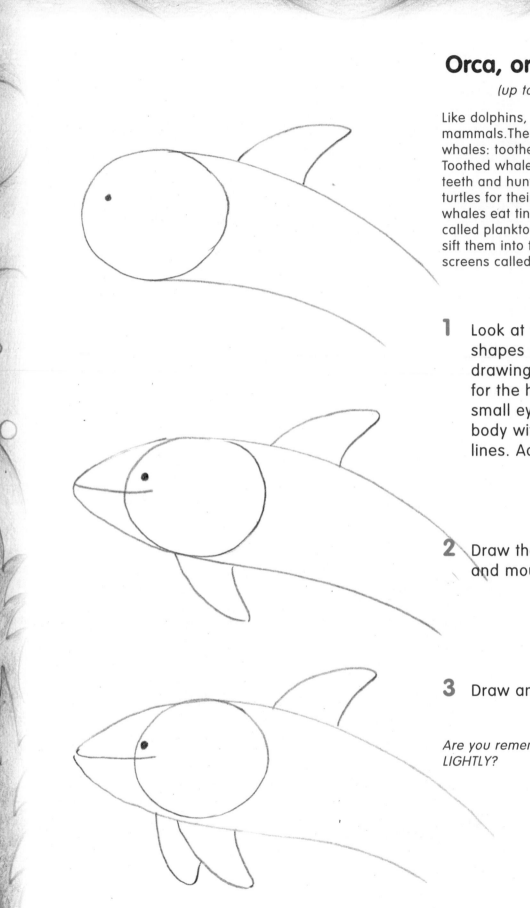

1 Look at the lines and shapes in the first drawing. Sketch an oval for the head. Draw a small eye. Begin Orca's body with two curved lines. Add a dorsal fin.

2 Draw the whale's snout and mouth. Add a flipper.

3 Draw another flipper.

Are you remembering to SKETCH LIGHTLY?

7

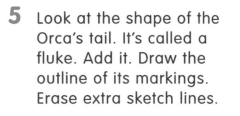

5 Look at the shape of the
Orca's tail. It's called a
fluke. Add it. Draw the
outline of its markings.
Erase extra sketch lines.

6 Look at the final drawing.
Add shading and color.

*When whales leap out of the
water, it is called 'breaching'.*

Humpback Whale

(up to 60 feet long)

Humpbacks are baleen whales. They eat a thousand pounds of krill (tiny shrimp) and plankton every day. They live in groups called pods. Humpbacks have extra long flippers that they like to use to smack the surface of the water. They speak to each other with long, complicated patterns of tones called 'songs'.

1 Look at the beginning shapes. Sketch an oval for the body. On one side of the oval, draw the shape of the head. On the other side of the oval, start the tail.

2 Draw the whale's tail flukes. Draw the flipper.

3 Draw a dorsal fin. Add an eye. Notice the way the mouth curves. Draw it.

9

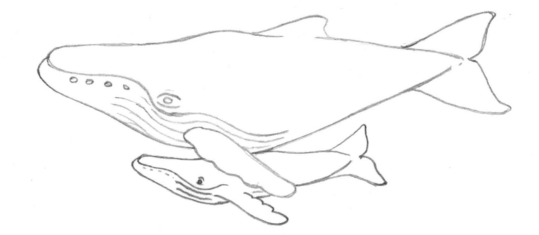

5 Erase extra sketch lines. Add markings under the mouth and on the whale's belly. Draw the whale's calf, but make it smaller than the mother whale.

6 Look at the final drawing. Shade and color your whales.

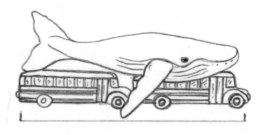

Sea Turtle

(2 to 6 feet long)

Sea turtles are reptiles. They live in the ocean and rise to the surface to breathe air through their nostrils. Females swim back to the beaches where they were hatched to lay their eggs. Sea turtles can live very long lives. Some are known to be over a hundred years old.

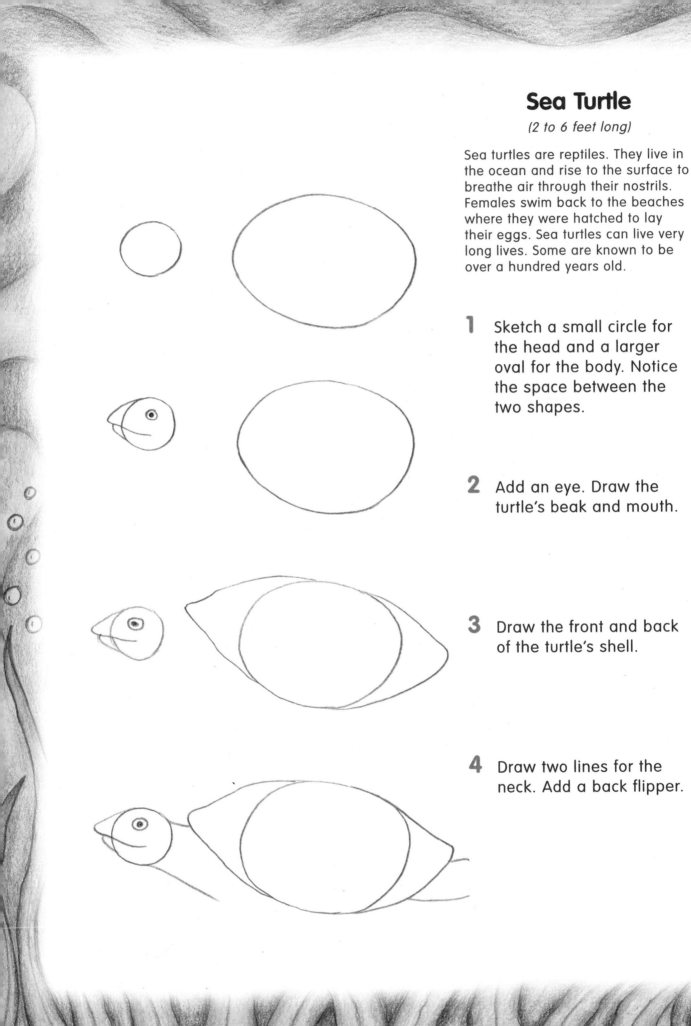

1 Sketch a small circle for the head and a larger oval for the body. Notice the space between the two shapes.

2 Add an eye. Draw the turtle's beak and mouth.

3 Draw the front and back of the turtle's shell.

4 Draw two lines for the neck. Add a back flipper.

5 Draw two front flippers. Erase extra sketch lines.

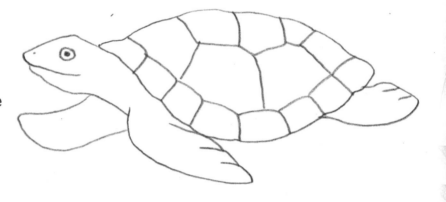

6 Look at the pattern on the turtle's shell. Using curved lines, draw the pattern. Add lines to the flippers. Draw a nostril.

7 Look at the final drawing. Shade and color your turtle.

Terrific Turtle!

Squid

(1 inch or up to 60 feet long!)

Squid are not fish and do not have a backbone. They can swim very fast by squirting jets of water behind them. They can change color to hide from enemies. If you threaten or startle a squid, it will squirt black ink at you.

1 Look at the shapes that begin the squid. Start with an oval for the body and a circle for the head. Notice how they overlap.

2 Sketch a triangle beak. Draw two ovals to begin the eye.

3 Erase extra sketch lines. Finish the eye.

4 Look at the four tentacles. Using curved lines, draw these.

13

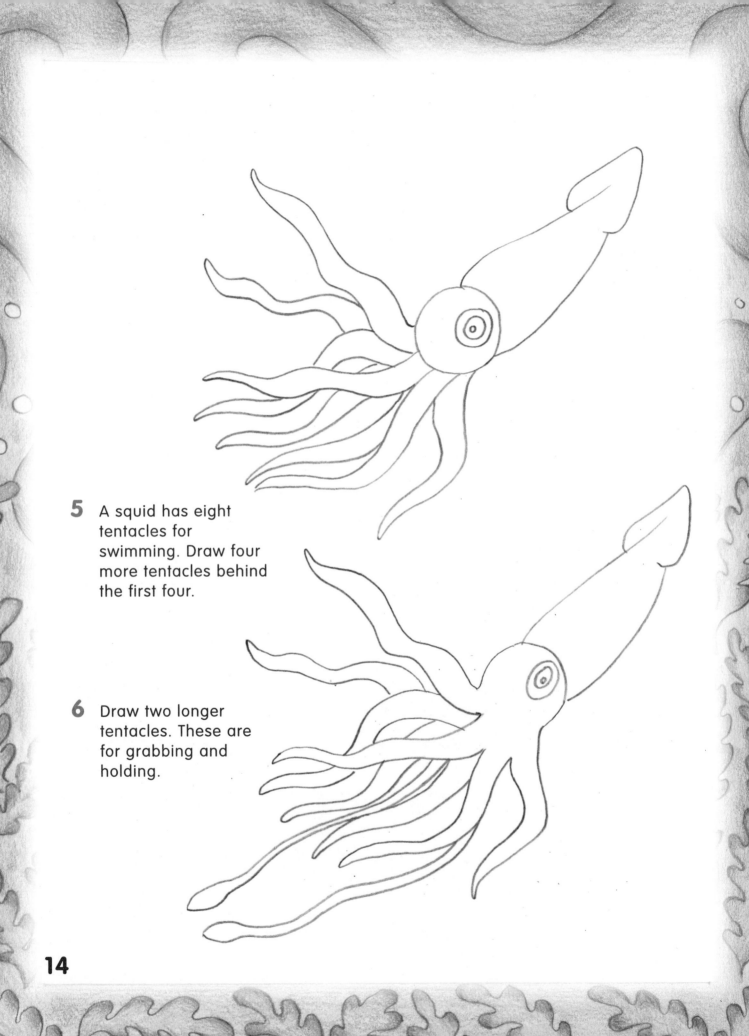

5 A squid has eight
tentacles for
swimming. Draw four
more tentacles behind
the first four.

6 Draw two longer
tentacles. These are
for grabbing and
holding.

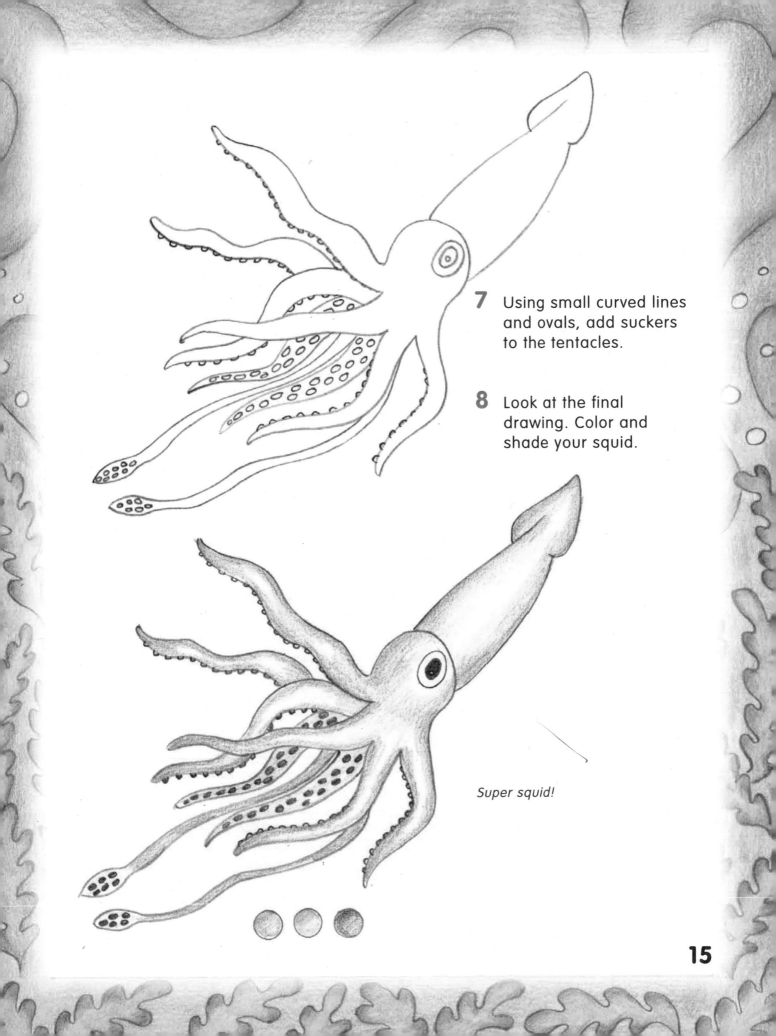

7 Using small curved lines and ovals, add suckers to the tentacles.

8 Look at the final drawing. Color and shade your squid.

Super squid!

Octopus

(3/8 of an inch to 23 feet)

An octopus is a cousin to a squid. Its name means 'eight feet'. Shy octopi like to stay close to the sea bed. They have large brains and are very intelligent. They have good eyesight but cannot hear. Like squid, they can change color and squirt black ink. Their blood is blue! If an octopus loses a tentacle, it can grow a new one.

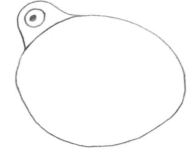

1 Look at the beginning drawing. Sketch an oval for the body. Draw a curved bump on the oval. Put an eye inside the bump.

2 Start two tentacles with curved lines.

3 Using more curved lines, finish the two tentacles. Start the next tentacle with a short, curly line.

4 Finish the short tentacle. Using curved lines, start two more.

5 Finish the next two tentacles and add suckers. Erase extra lines. An octopus has eight tentacles but you cannot see all of them at once in most positions. Draw small ovals on the body oval.

6 Look at the final drawing. Shade and color your octopus.

Awesome octopus!

Crab

(a few inches to 12 feet across)

Crabs do not have backbones. They have a hard outer shell called an exoskeleton. Most crabs live in the ocean and like to hide in the sand. When they walk, they walk sideways.

1 Look at the shape that begins this drawing. Sketch a trapezoid.

2 Using curved lines, round off the corners of the trapezoid. Erase the extra sketch lines.

3 Starting at the top, draw two round bumps for eyes. Using curved lines, draw two shapes to begin the crab's pincers. On the bottom and sides, draw the shapes to begin eight jointed legs.

4 Look at the pincers. Add additional sections to the crab's pincers. Look at the legs. Add the next section to all eight legs.

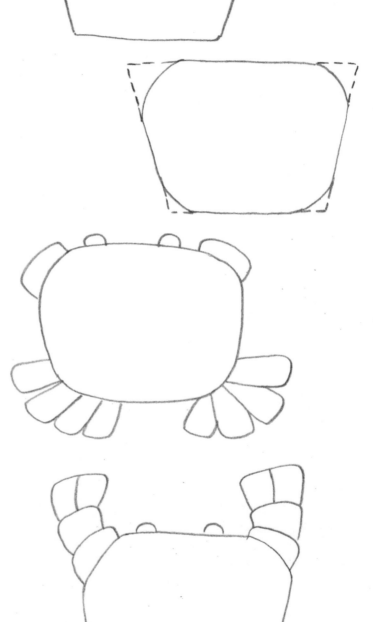

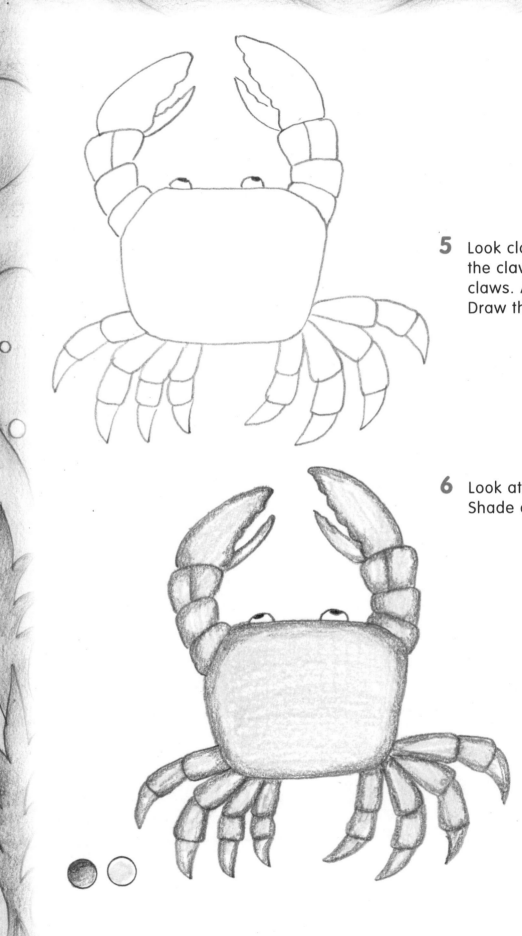

5 Look closely at the shape of the claws. Draw the two claws. Add two eyeballs. Draw the eight feet.

6 Look at the final drawing. Shade and color your crab.

Shrimp

(from a fraction of an inch to about 8 inches long)

Shrimp are in the same family as crabs and lobsters. They live on the ocean floor and eat small plants and animals. They have legs for walking and when they want to swim, they use their swimmerets.

1   Sketch an oval for the body.

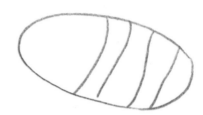

2   Draw lines on the oval to show the shrimp's segmented body.

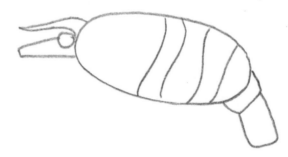

3   Look at the shape of the feeler, the shrimp's snout, and eye. Draw the shapes you see. Using curved lines, begin the first two sections of the tail.

4   Darken part of the eye. Add two points to the snout. Look at the parts of the feeler. Draw these. Add the beginning of the shrimp's walking legs. Finish the sections of the tail.

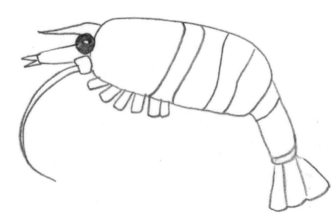

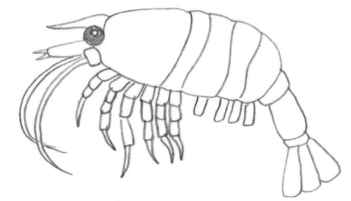

5 Draw another long feeler. Add sections to the walking legs. Begin the swimmerets.

6 Draw the last section of the four swimmerets.

7 Look at the final drawing. Color and shade your shrimp.

Starfish

(average size is a few inches)

A starfish is not a fish. It is a spiny, hard skinned animal that lives on the rocky sea bed. Most have five arms which can regrow if lost. Starfish eat mussels and clams. Sometimes they are called Sea Stars.

1 Start by sketching a triangle.

2 Sketch two more triangles. Notice the angle of the triangles.

3 Add two more triangles.

4 Erase extra sketch lines. Go over the outline with jagged pencil strokes. Draw a dot in the center of the starfish. Draw a line from the base of each triangle to the center of the starfish. Draw a line from each point to the center dot. Using short pencil strokes, add a bumpy texture to the starfish.

5 Shade and color your starfish.

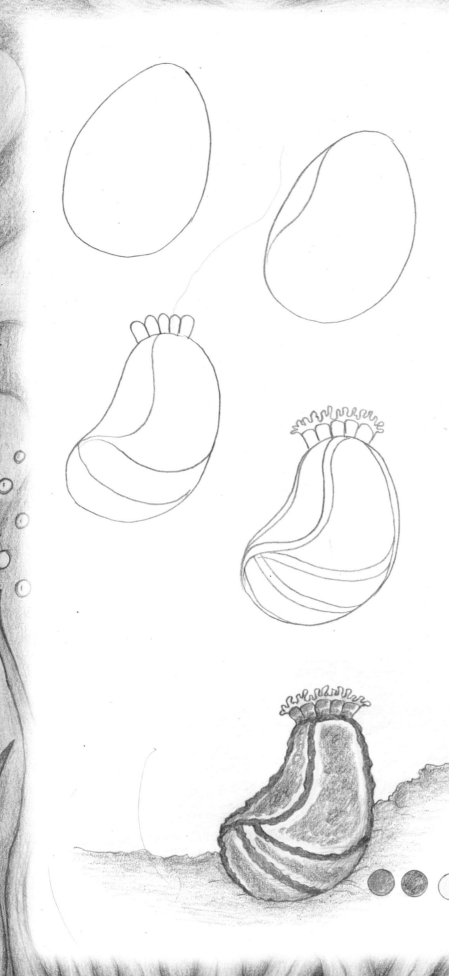

Sea Cucumber

(a few inches long)

A sea cucumber is a cousin to the starfish. It moves very, very slowly. It sucks in food that sticks to its tentacles then pulls the tentacles into its body. It lives on the sea bed.

1 Sketch an egg shape to begin.

2 Make the egg shaped more like a bean by drawing a curved line on one side.

3 Look at the sea cucumber's shape now. Erase the extra outer sketch line. Draw three more curved lines on the body. Begin the tentacles with five small bumps.

4 Add tentacles to the bumps. Double the lines you drew on the body of the sea cucumber.

5 Look at the final drawing. Shade and color your sea cucumber very brightly.

Cool cucumber!

Jellyfish

(a few inches to over three feet long)

A jellyfish is not a fish but a very ancient and simple creature. It has no brain, no bones, no eyes, and no heart. It is mostly water. Jellyfish float near the surface and move by opening and closing its body which is called a bell. Most have long tentacles which can give a painful and even deadly sting.

1 Look at the beginning shapes. Sketch a circle. To make the shape of the bell, draw curved lines on both sides of the circle.

2 Draw the first two 'arms' of the jellyfish.

3 Erase extra sketch lines in the bell. Draw a curved line inside the bell with three bumps. Using short curved lines, go over and shape the bottom bell line. Add another arm.

4 Add another line inside the bell. Draw the first four tentacles.

5 Add a small curved triangle near the bell top. Leave it white to show the shininess of the jellyfish. Look at the three additional tentacles. Add these.

6 Look at the final drawing. Shade and color your jellyfish. To show that it is transparent, color it very delicately.

Sea shells

(one to three inches)

Sea shells are houses for soft bodied ocean animals. A sand dollar is a relative of a spiny sea urchin. When these shells wash up onto the shore, they dry out and bleach in the sun.

Scallop

1 Sketch a triangle.
2 Sketch a half circle on top of the triangle. Add two triangles at the bottom of the shell.
3 Look at the final drawing. Erase extra lines. Add curved lines on top. Draw lines for the ribs. Add shading and color.

Whelk

1 Sketch a small rectangle.
2 Look at the added shapes. Draw these.
3 Add three more rectangles (each getting smaller than the last). Draw a line along the side of the shell.
4 Look at the final drawing. Add shading and color.

Sand Dollar

1 Sketch a circle.
2 Draw the flower shape in the center of the sand dollar. Add five small rectangular holes.
3 Look at the details in the final drawing. Color and shade your sand dollar.

26

Plankton

(as tiny as a letter on this page)

Plankton are tiny little animals that live near the surface of the ocean. They need sunlight to grow. They don't swim but move in large drifts than can number in the billions. They provide food for much larger ocean animals. A baleen whale can eat a thousand pounds of plankton every day. They are very small but they are an important link in the ocean food chain.

Look at these different shaped plankton. These drawings are larger than the actual plankton. Can you draw some of these shapes?

Shark

(12 to 16 feet long)

A shark is an ancient fish. There have been sharks swimming in the ocean for millions of years, looking very much the same as they are now. There are three hundred kinds of sharks but not all of them are dangerous. Sharks are strong swimmers with an excellent sense of smell. Great White sharks are the fiercest.

1 Notice the angle of the body oval. Sketch it lightly to begin the shark's body.

2 Draw the pointy shape of the shark's nose. Sketch the curved shape to begin the tail.

3 Draw an eye and a mouth. Draw the dorsal fin. Draw two pelvic fins. Add two anal fins. Continue drawing the tail by adding a small triangle.

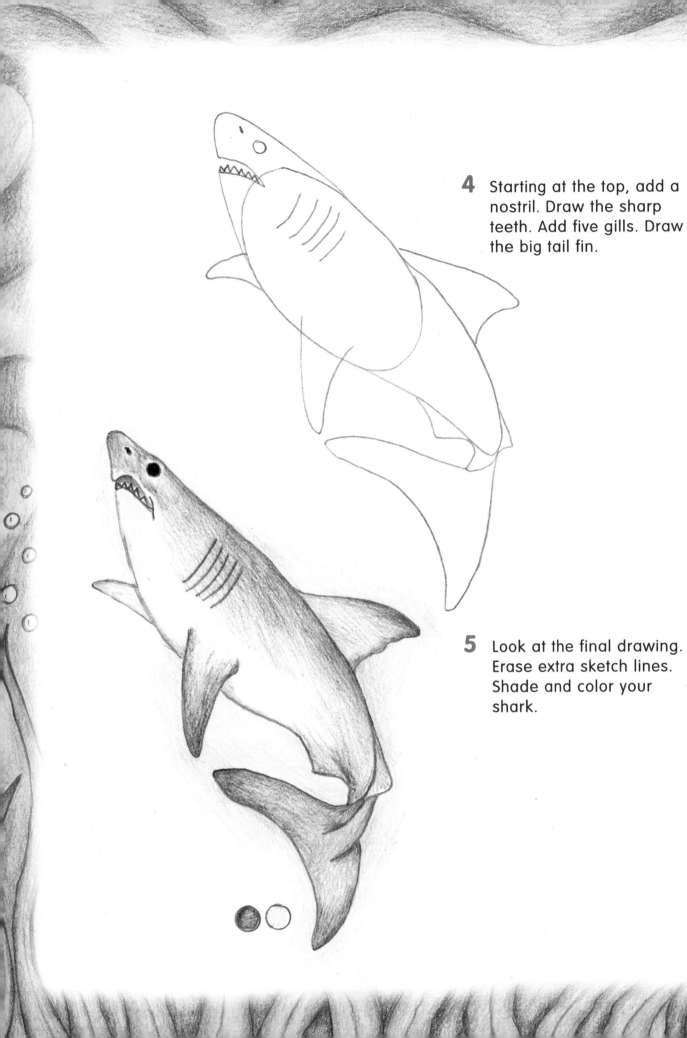

4 Starting at the top, add a nostril. Draw the sharp teeth. Add five gills. Draw the big tail fin.

5 Look at the final drawing. Erase extra sketch lines. Shade and color your shark.

Hammerhead Shark

(up to 12 feet)

The Hammerhead Shark has an oddly shaped head. Its eyes are on the side of its rectangular skull. Hammerheads swim in large schools. They live in warm water and have an excellent sense of smell.

1 Sketch a circle to begin the head.

2 Add two rectangles on each side of the circle.

3 Start drawing the body with two long, curving lines. Draw two pelvic fins. Add another pelvic fin. Draw an eye.

4 Draw the triangular dorsal fin. Add two anal fins.

5 Using curved lines, add the tail fin. Draw four gills. Erase extra sketch lines.

6 Look at the final drawing. Shade and color your hammerhead shark.

Ray

(4 inches to 22 feet)

Gentle rays are cousins of sharks. They are flat fish that swim along the sea floor, eating plankton with mouths that are on the underside of their bodies.

1   Sketch an oval to begin the ray's body. Notice the angle of the oval.

2   Draw two curved triangle shapes on either side of the oval.

3   Draw a small curved nose and two eyes. Draw a circle between the two triangle shapes.

4   Add a long, pointed, curved tail. Erase extra lines.

32

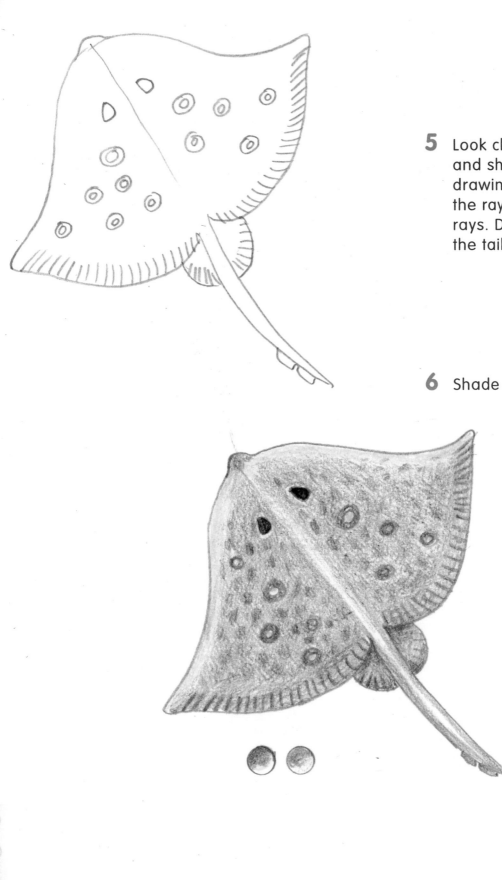

5 Look closely at the lines and shapes added in this drawing. Draw spots on the ray's back. Add fin rays. Draw two barbs on the tail.

6 Shade and color your ray.

Anglerfish

(only 5 inches long)

The anglerfish is a real trickster. It lives in the very deep part of the ocean where there is little light. It has a glowing ball on the end of a spine that attracts fish and lures them. When they get close to the light, the anglerfish gobbles them up!

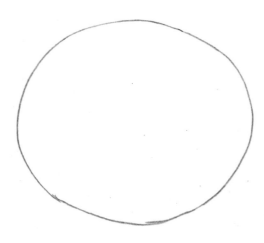

1 Sketch a nice fat circle.

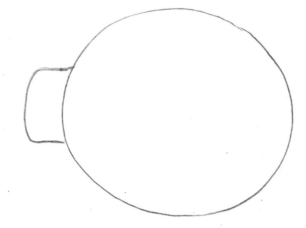

2 Add a rectangle for the base of the tail.

3 Draw the tail fin and add two more fins on each side of it.

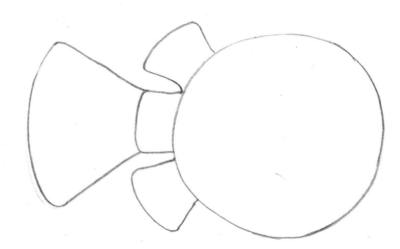

4 Add a pectoral fin. Look closely at the 'Z' shaped line. Draw this to begin the snout and open mouth.

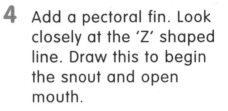

5 Using two curved lines, begin the spine above the snout. Draw an eye. Add jagged teeth. Draw a curved line to complete the jaw.

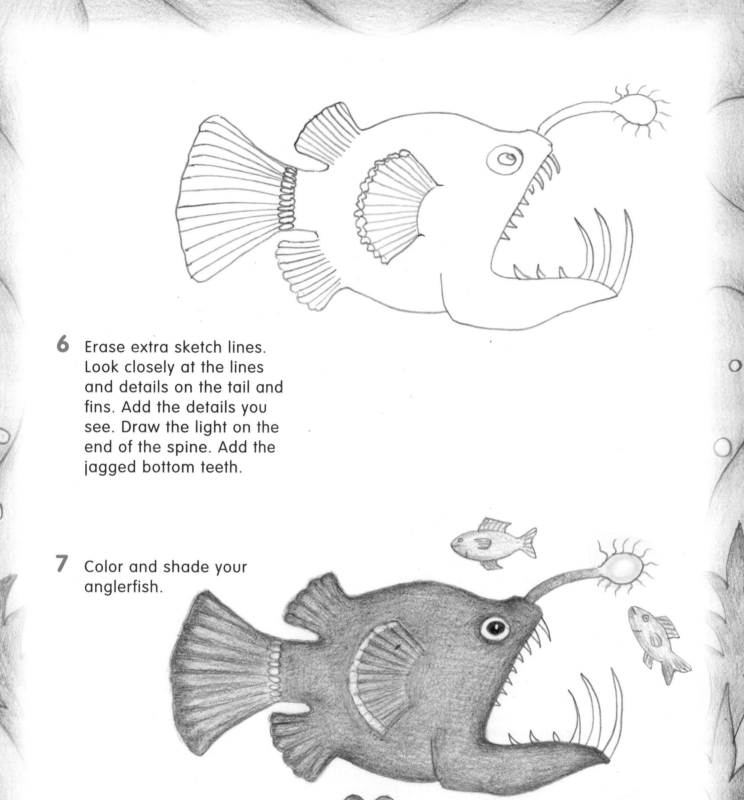

6 Erase extra sketch lines. Look closely at the lines and details on the tail and fins. Add the details you see. Draw the light on the end of the spine. Add the jagged bottom teeth.

7 Color and shade your anglerfish.

Awesome!

Eel

(3 to 5 feet long)

An eel looks like a snake, but it is a fish. Eels like to hide in the cracks between rocks. They wait for smaller fish to swim by, then grab them with their sharp teeth. Young eels are called 'elvers'.

1 Sketch a tilted oval for the head.

2 Draw a slightly curved triangle to begin the mouth. Start the body with two curved lines that come to a point.

3 Draw the eye. Add a line inside the mouth.

4 Add sharp teeth. Draw a long, thin dorsal fin.

5 Add the rest of the tail with two long curving lines that come to a point. Erase extra lines.

6 Look closely at the shading and color in the final drawing. Shade and color lightly at first, then add more gradually.

Extraordinary eel!

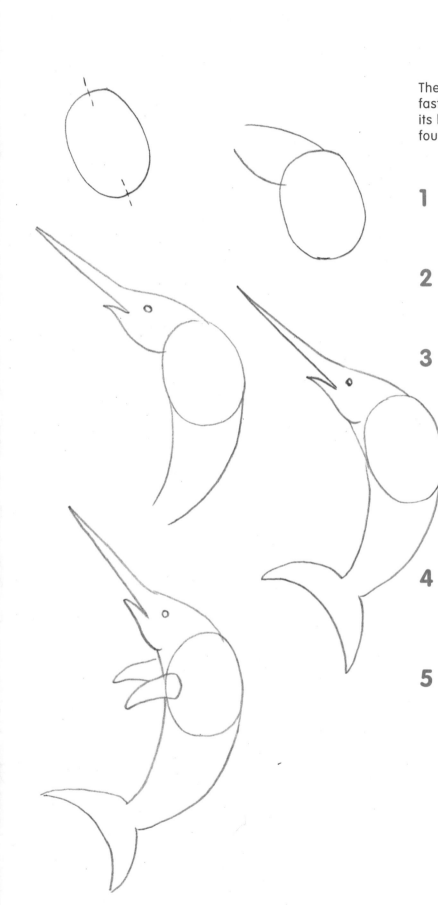

Swordfish
(up to 15 feet long)

The swordfish is a strong fish and a fast swimmer. Its name comes from its long, sharp bill. Swordfish are found all over the world.

1 Sketch an oval to begin the body.

2 Draw two curved lines to begin the head.

3 Add the long, sharp bill and the lower jaw. Draw an eye. Draw two curved lines to begin the tail.

4 Draw a line connecting the head with the body. Add the tail fin.

5 Draw two pelvic fins.

6 Erase extra sketch lines. Add the pelvic fin. Draw two anal fins.

7 Draw the dorsal fin and the lateral line.

8 Look at the final drawing. Shade and color your swordfish.

Super swordfish!

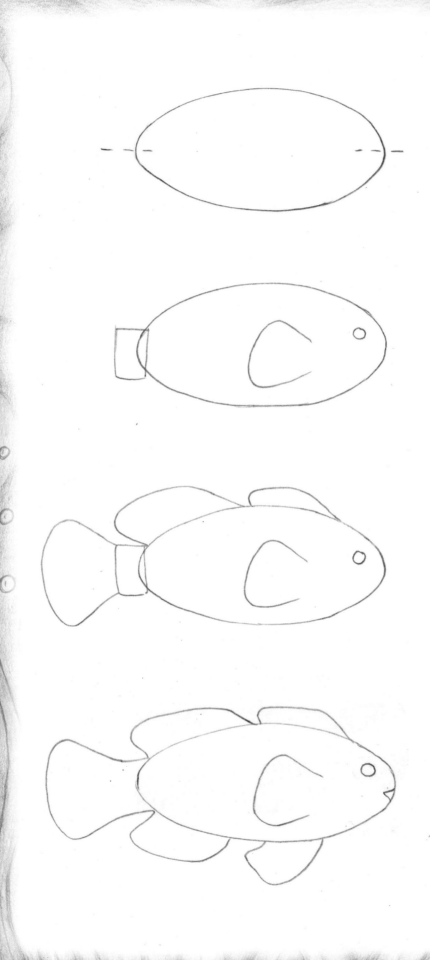

Clown fish
(2 or 3 inches)

Clown fish live among the stinging tentacles of sea anemones (see page 43). They have a special slimy coating on their bodies that keeps them from being hurt. Inside the anemone, they are safe from other fish that might want to eat them.

1 Sketch an oval.

2 Sketch a rectangle for the base of the tail. Draw the pectoral fin. Add an eye.

3 Draw two dorsal fins. Complete the tail with a trapezoid shape.

4 Draw the pelvic and anal fins. Add a mouth. Erase extra sketch lines.

5 Look at the outline of the clown fish's markings. Draw the lines you see.

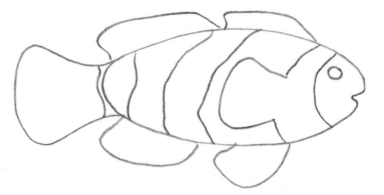

6 Add the fin rays.

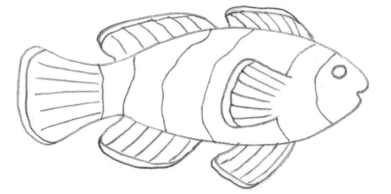

7 Look at the final drawing. Shade and color your bright orange clown fish.

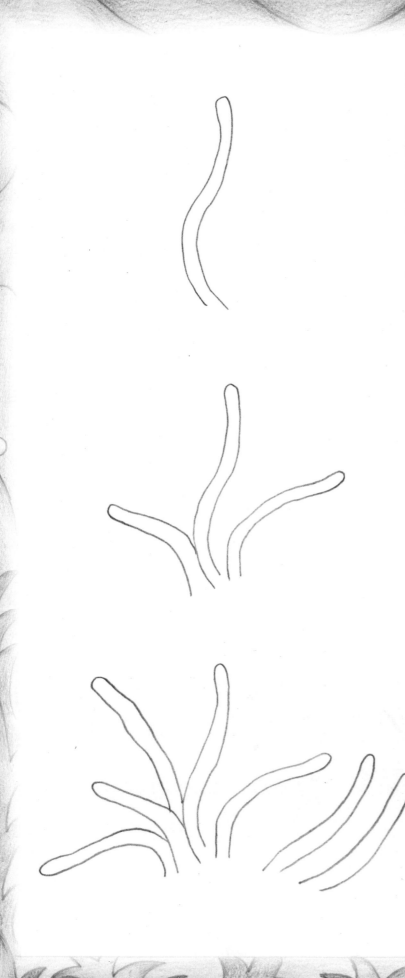

Sea Anemone *(uh NEM in ee)*

(1 to 4 inches across)

Sea anemones look like ocean flowers, but they are animals. They capture small fish and other animals that stray too close to their stinging, waving tentacles. They live on the sea floor of warm, tropical coral reefs. (See pages 62 -63.)

1 Sketch one tube shaped tentacle to begin.

2 Add two more tentacles.

3 Draw four more tentacles. Make them curve in different ways.

4 Add more tentacles. Let them overlap each other. Using little squiggly lines, make tips on the end of the tentacles.

5 Look at the final drawing. Add color and shade. Draw a clown fish hiding between the tentacles.

Sea Horse

(1 to 5 inches)

Shy little sea horse is an unusual fish. The male sea horse carries the baby sea horses inside his body in a special pouch. The pouch gets rounder and rounder until the babies are big enough to survive. Then the pouch opens and the babies spill out into the water. Sea horses can change colors to blend with their surroundings.

1 Sketch an oval for the body and a smaller circle for the head. Notice the positions of both shapes.

2 Draw the back of the head and neck with two curving lines. Look closely at the shape of the top line. Draw the sea horse's snout. It's shaped like a horse's muzzle. Add an eye.

3 To start the tail, draw a curving line that ends in a curl.

45

4 Finish the tail with a second curving line. Draw a dorsal fin. Add a curving line down the inside of the sea horses body. Draw spiky fins all down the back of the sea horse.

5 Erase extra lines. Draw the armor-like plates on the sea horse's body.

6 Shade and color your sea horse. Draw a piece of sea weed or coral for it to wind its tail around.

Sweet sea horse!

Pipefish

(3 to 6 inches)

Pipefish are cousins of sea horses. Their long, thin shape and banded markings help them blend into their surroundings.

1 Sketch a long thin rectangle to begin the pipefish.

2 Draw the head and snout. Add a small trapezoid to begin the tail.

3 Draw an eye. Add a tail.

4 Draw the banded stripes.

5 Look at the final drawing. Shade and color your pipefish.

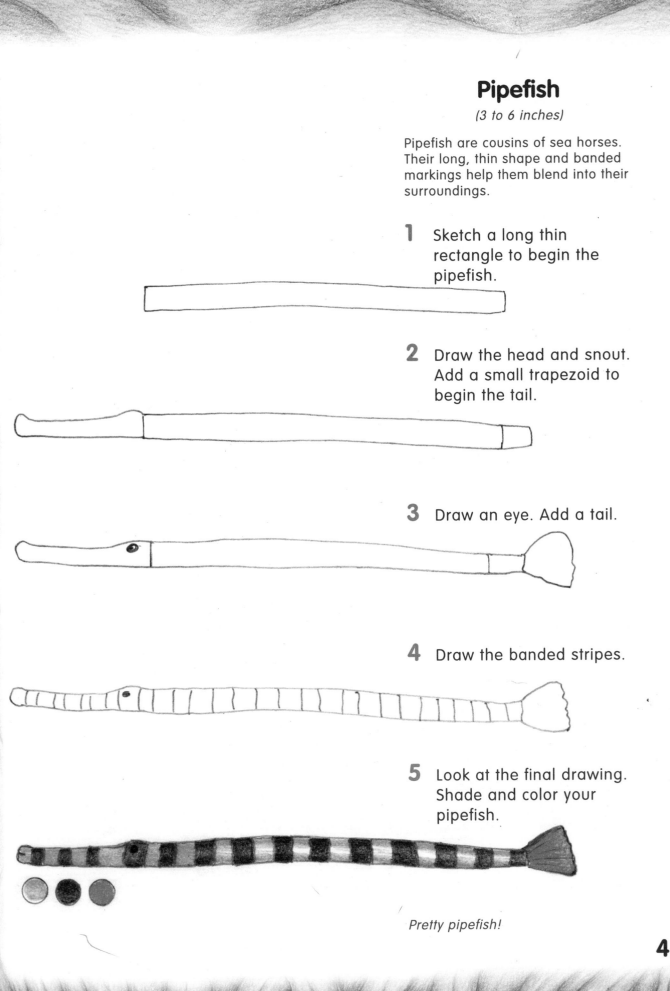

Pretty pipefish!

47

Puffer fish

(3 - 20 inches)

A puffer fish has a good trick. When it's relaxed, its spines are flat against its body. When it's threatened, it swallows water and puffs up like a round balloon to almost twice its size. It becomes too big and prickly for other fish to swallow.

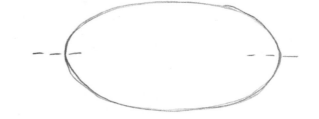

1 Let's draw the puffer fish both ways. Sketch an oval to begin the relaxed puffer fish.

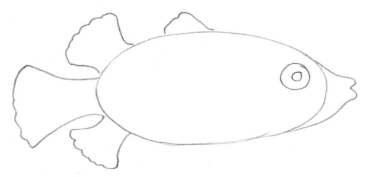

2 Add the mouth. Draw an eye. Add a dorsal fin. Draw the tail fin and two anal fins.

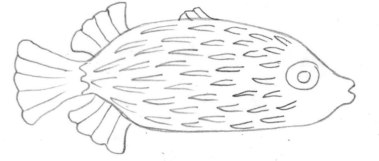

3 Erase extra lines. Draw the fin rays. Add the spines, flat against the fish's body.

4 Look at the final drawing. Shade and color your relaxed puffer fish.

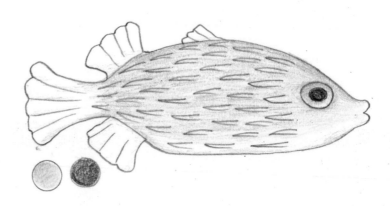

Puffer fish - puffed up

1 Draw a circle. Don't forget, draw lightly! Add two fins. Draw two round eyes and an oval shaped mouth. Draw a tiny top tooth in the mouth.

2 Add the fin rays. Draw the spines standing straight out from the puffer fish's body.

3 Look at the final drawing. Shade and color your puffed up puffer fish. Wonder what scared him?

Blue Tang

(6 to 12 inches)

The blue tang is a peaceful tropical fish with pretty black, blue, and yellow markings. It likes to live near branching coral and eats plankton and tiny plants.

1 Sketch an oval.

2 Draw an eye and a mouth. Add a pectoral fin. Draw the tail fin.

3 Add a long thin dorsal fin. Look at the tang's markings Using curved lines, draw these.

4 Look at the brilliant colors. Shade and color your Blue Tang.

Terrific Tang!

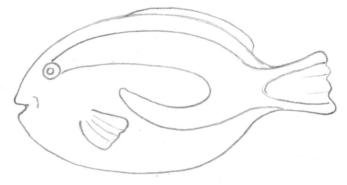

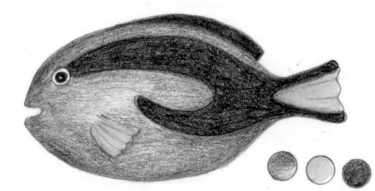

50

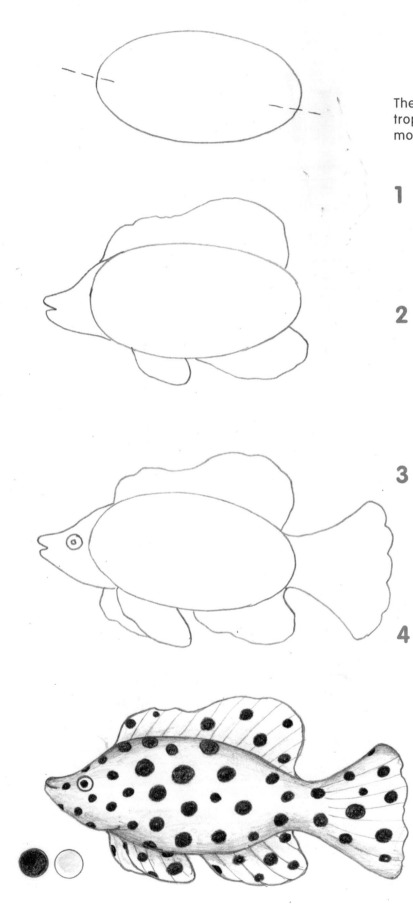

Polkadot Grouper

(12 to 20 inches)

The Polkadot Grouper is a graceful tropical fish that is constantly on the move.

1 Sketch an oval for the body.

2 Draw the snout and mouth. Add a large dorsal fin. Notice the shape. Draw a pelvic fin and an anal fin.

3 Add an eye. Add a second pelvic fin. Draw the tail fin.

4 Look at the final drawing. Erase extra sketch lines. Add fin rays and its fabulous polkadots. Shade your drawing.

Great Grouper!

51

Long-nosed Butterfly Fish

(7 inches)

This pretty fish swims in the Indian Ocean. It uses its long nose to pull small creatures out of cracks and crevices in rocks.

1   Lightly sketch an oval.

2   Add the Butterfly fish's long snout. Draw an eye. Add a dorsal fin. Draw the tail fin. Draw the two fins along its belly.

3   Add the fin rays on the tail, and the stripes.

4   Look at the final drawing. Erase extra sketch lines. Shade and color your fish.

Brilliant!

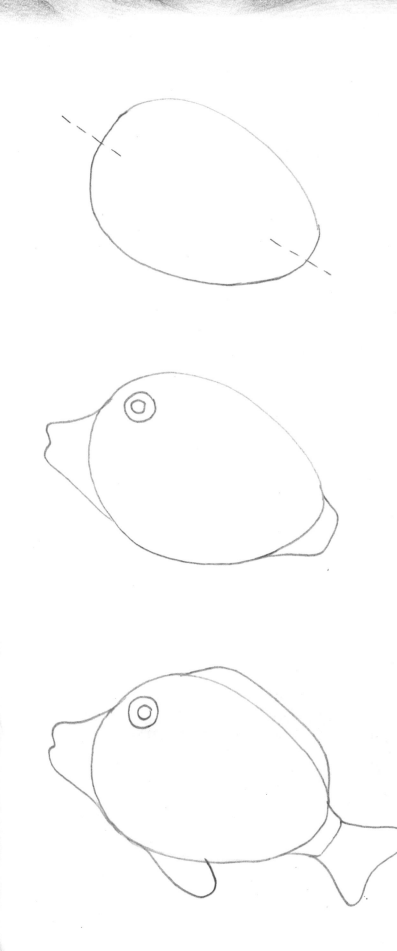

Powder Blue Tang
(5 to 9 inches)

The Powder Blue Tang is another really beautiful fish with vivid colors and bold markings. Its very active and feeds on algae.

1 Sketch an egg shape to begin. Notice the angle of the egg.

2 Draw the fish's snout. Add an eye. Draw the beginning of the tail.

3 Add a long thin dorsal fin. Draw the tail fin. Add a pelvic fin.

4 Draw fin rays. Add a second pelvic fin and an anal fin. Draw the pectoral fin.

5 Erase extra lines. Draw the fish's markings. Add the remaining fin rays.

6 Look at the final drawing. Shade and color your Powder Blue Tang.

On a deeply colored fish like this, add color gradually until the blue is very bright and the black markings are really dark.

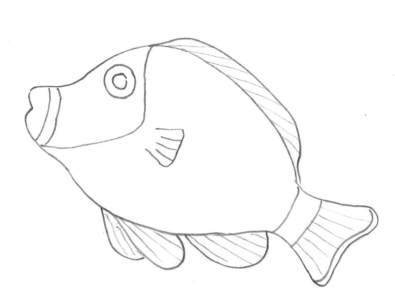

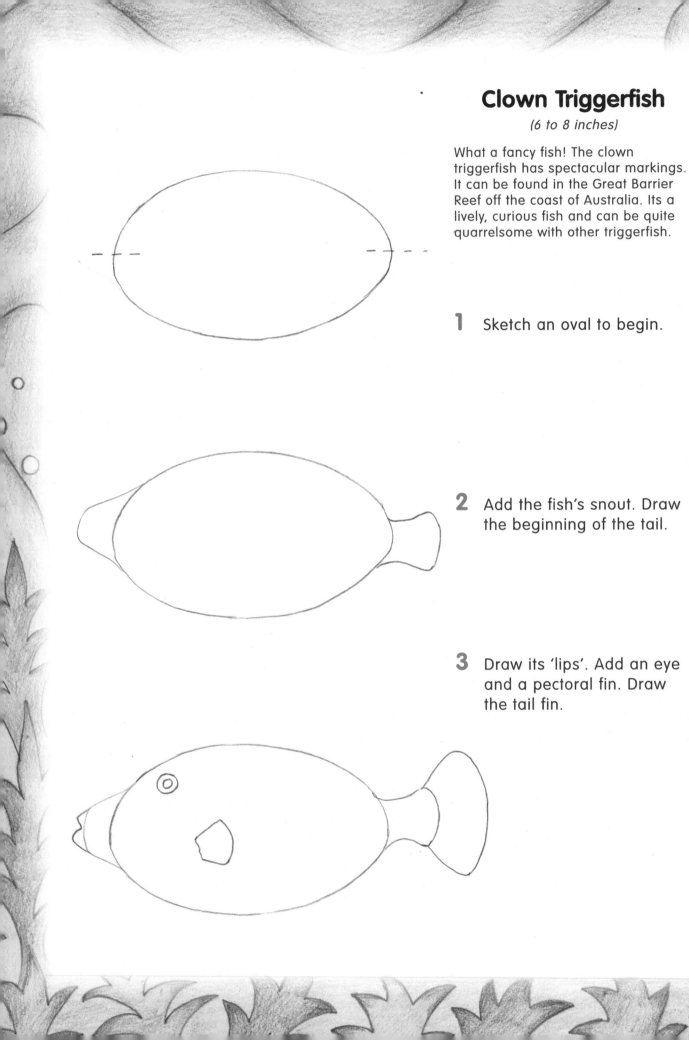

Clown Triggerfish
(6 to 8 inches)

What a fancy fish! The clown triggerfish has spectacular markings. It can be found in the Great Barrier Reef off the coast of Australia. Its a lively, curious fish and can be quite quarrelsome with other triggerfish.

1 Sketch an oval to begin.

2 Add the fish's snout. Draw the beginning of the tail.

3 Draw its 'lips'. Add an eye and a pectoral fin. Draw the tail fin.

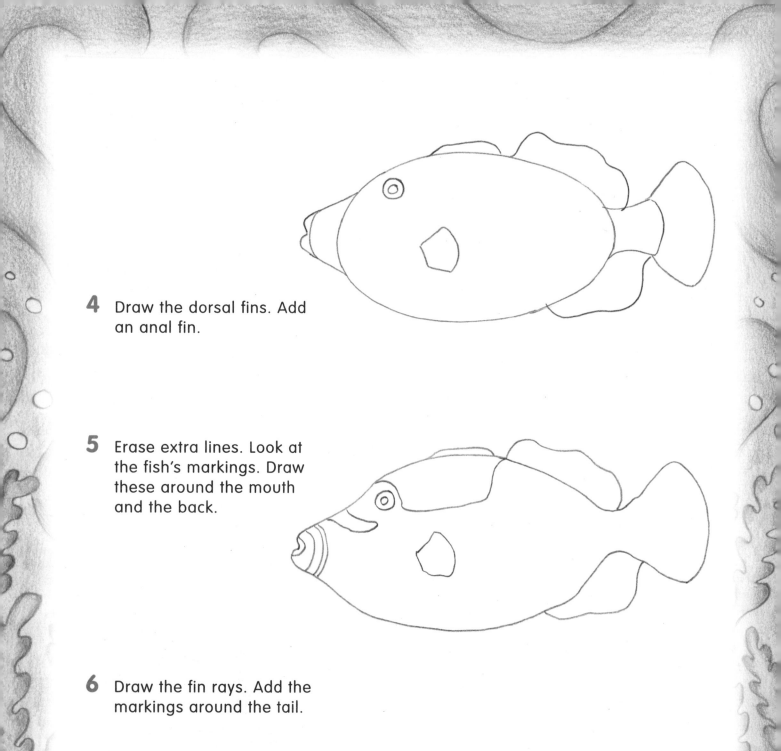

4 Draw the dorsal fins. Add an anal fin.

5 Erase extra lines. Look at the fish's markings. Draw these around the mouth and the back.

6 Draw the fin rays. Add the markings around the tail.

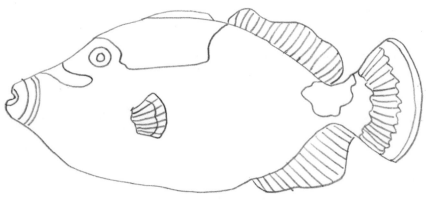

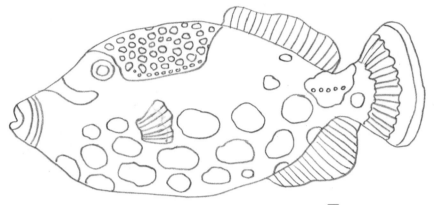

7 Draw the small dots on top. Draw big dots on the side and bottom.

8 Look at the final drawing. Shade and color your Clown Triggerfish

Lion fish

(8 to 15 inches)

The lion fish is an amazing-looking tropical fish with lots of graceful, frilly spines. It is a rather dangerous fish as its spines are poisonous. It's a bit complicated to draw, but we will go slowly.

1 Sketch an egg shape to begin.

2 Draw the fish's snout and mouth. Add the beginning of the tail.

3 Notice how the eye is placed on the fish's head. Draw it. Add the spiky dorsal fins. Complete the tail fin.

4 Look closely at the emerging shapes. Draw barbels around the eye and chin. Add a dorsal fin. Draw two sets of spines on the fish's belly.

5 Now draw a set of pectoral spines on the side of the fish.

6 Erase extra sketch lines.

7 Look closely at the coloring of the markings on the fish's head, fins, and tail. Color these. Add bars to the eye ring and the barbels on the fish's head.

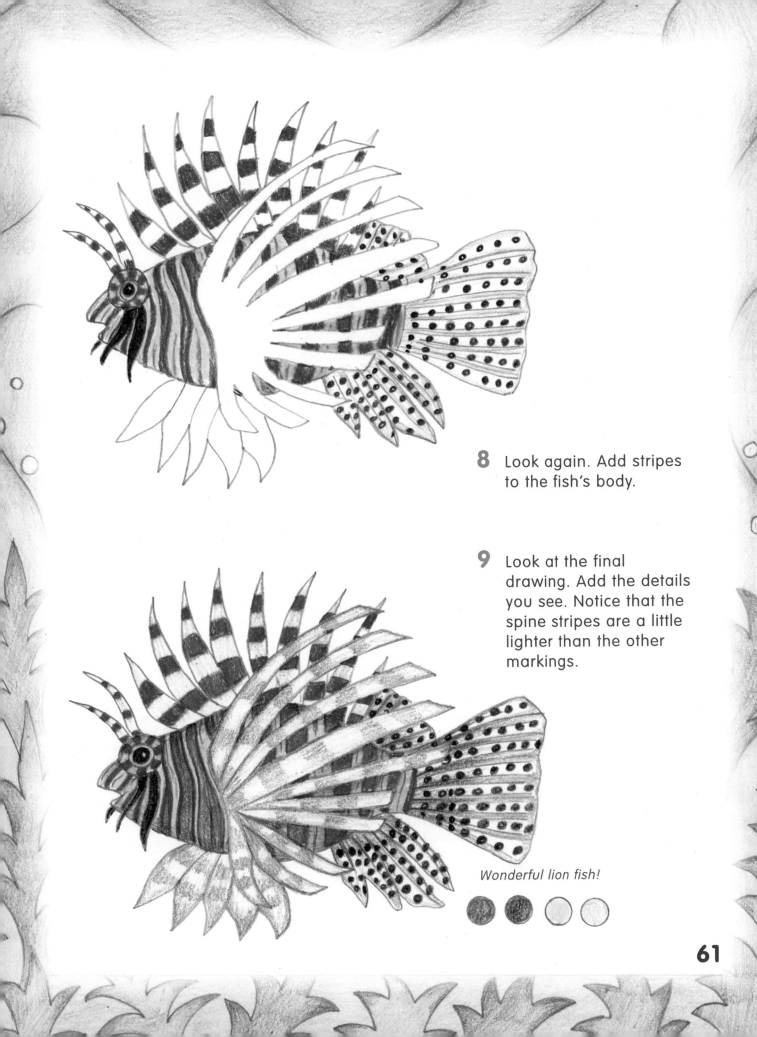

8 Look again. Add stripes to the fish's body.

9 Look at the final drawing. Add the details you see. Notice that the spine stripes are a little lighter than the other markings.

Wonderful lion fish!

Coral and coral reefs

Coral reefs are warm, shallow areas of the ocean that are full of beautiful fish and sea creatures. The reefs are built by tiny, primitive animals called polyps. The polyps live in chalky shelters that protect their soft bodies. As they die, their skeletons are added to the reef. It slowly grows, one layer on top of another, adding about an inch a year. The Great Barrier Reef, off of the coast of Australia is 1200 miles long. It is so big, it can be seen from space.

Coral comes in many shapes and colors. Look closely at these drawings. Practice drawing some coral. Put them together with some of the fish and other creatures you have learned to draw to create a coral reef scene.

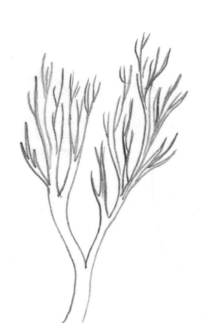

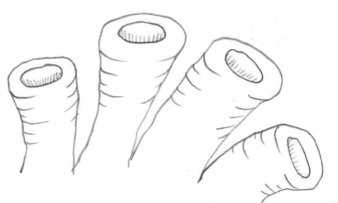

Index

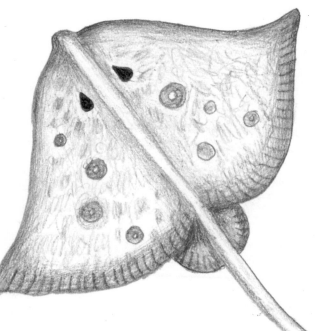

Learn about other
drawing books online at
www.drawbooks.com